The Traveling Kittens series follows Buffy and Sissy as they explore the world with their mama. Learn about travel through the experiences of these adorable kittens and follow them as they discover new cultures and make new friends.

This is the first book in the series.
COMING SOON - *Buffy & Sissy Go to Hawaii!*

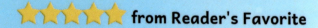 **from Reader's Favorite**

"Colleen Chapman's Buffy & Sissy Go to Italy will have young and grownup readers alike thinking wistfully about spaghetti, pizza, gelato, and the wondrous sights Buffy and Sissy see on their trip. Throughout the story, readers are also introduced to key words and phrases in Italian. Chapman's book educates as it entertains, which is what travel is about in so many ways. Pardeep Mehra's bright and cheerful illustrations make the kittens' experiences in Italy come to life. Buffy & Sissy Go to Italy: The Traveling Kittens, book one is most highly recommended!"

– Jack Magnus, *Reader's Favorite*

To follow Buffy & Sissy's travels, please visit
http://www.thetravelingkittens.com

This book belongs to:

Copyright © 2020 Colleen Chapman

All rights reserved. Without prior permission of the authors, no part of this publication may be reproduced, stored in a retrieval system, or transmitted in any form or by any means—electronic, mechanical, photocopy, recording, or any other— except for brief quotations in printed reviews.

ISBN: 978-1-7348258-0-0 (paperback)
978-1-7348258-1-7 (hardback)
978-1-7348258-2-4 (ebook)

Library of Congress Control Number: 2020905670

Publisher's Cataloging-in-Publication Data

Names: Chapman, Colleen, author. | Mehra, Pardeep, illustrator.
Title: Buffy and Sissy go to Italy / author: Colleen Chapman; illustrator: Pardeep Mehra.
Series: The Traveling Kittens
Description: | Summary: Buffy & Sissy, two traveling kittens, help children embrace travel and learn about Italy
Identifiers: LCCN: 2020905670 | ISBN: 978-1-7348258-1-7 (Hardcover) | 978-1-7348258-0-0 (pbk.) | 978-1-7348258-2-4 (ebook)
Subjects: LCSH Kittens--Juvenile fiction. | Italy--Juvenile fiction. | Kittens--Fiction. | Italy--Fiction. | BISAC JUVENILE FICTION / Animals / Cats | JUVENILE FICTION / People & Places / Europe | JUVENILE FICTION / Travel
Classification: LCC PZ7.1.C484 Buf 2020| DDC [E]--dc23

"It's vacation time! Yippee!"
Buffy is excited.
"Sissy, we are going to Italy!" she shouts.
"Let's get packing!"

"Don't forget your toothbrushes," says Mama. "You can each bring two books to read on the airplane. And Sissy, remember to bring your camera!"

The kittens stuff their backpacks. They are ready for the long flight to Italy.

Buffy is awake early the next day. "Before you know it we will be in Italy! I can almost taste the spaghetti," she says. Buffy is always hungry!

"Are we there yet?" Sissy asks, taking pictures through the airplane window.
"We will be landing soon," answers Mama.
Buffy yawns, murmuring, "I'm hungry."

Ciao bella," says the porter at the airport.
Mama said that means hello beautiful in Italian.
"Welcome to *Florence, Italy*," he adds.
The kittens thank him and Buffy asks,
"Do they sell spaghetti here?" The porter laughs.
"You will find many places to eat spaghetti in Italy."

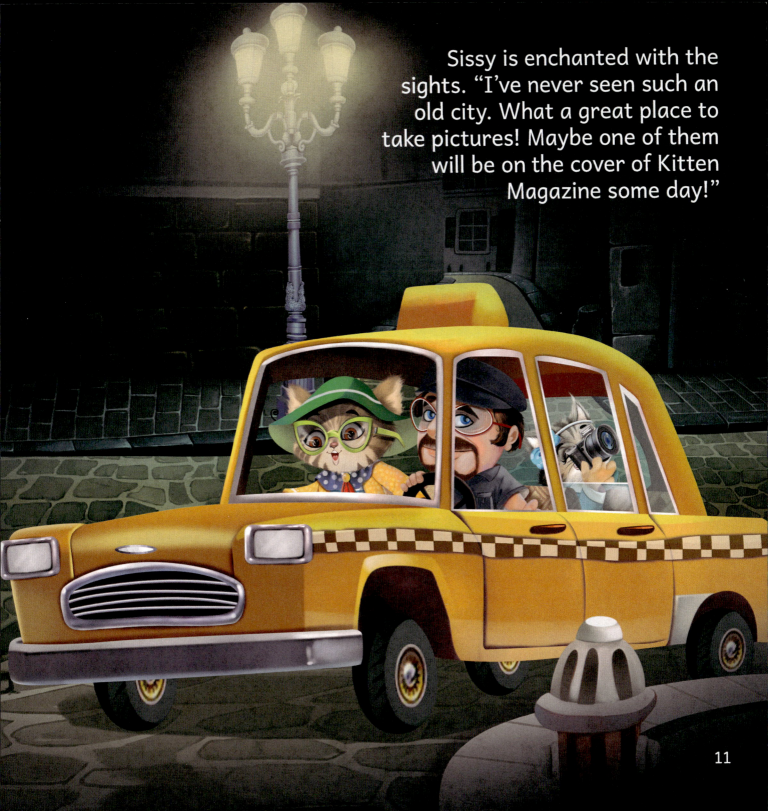

Sissy is enchanted with the sights. "I've never seen such an old city. What a great place to take pictures! Maybe one of them will be on the cover of Kitten Magazine some day!"

Setting out to explore the city, the kitties meet a friendly cat with long white whiskers. "Welcome to *Florence!* My name is Marcello. Where are you from?" he asks.
"We live in America," answers Buffy.
"Do you know where I can find spaghetti?"
Marcello replies with a wink.
"Food is my specialty. I can help you."

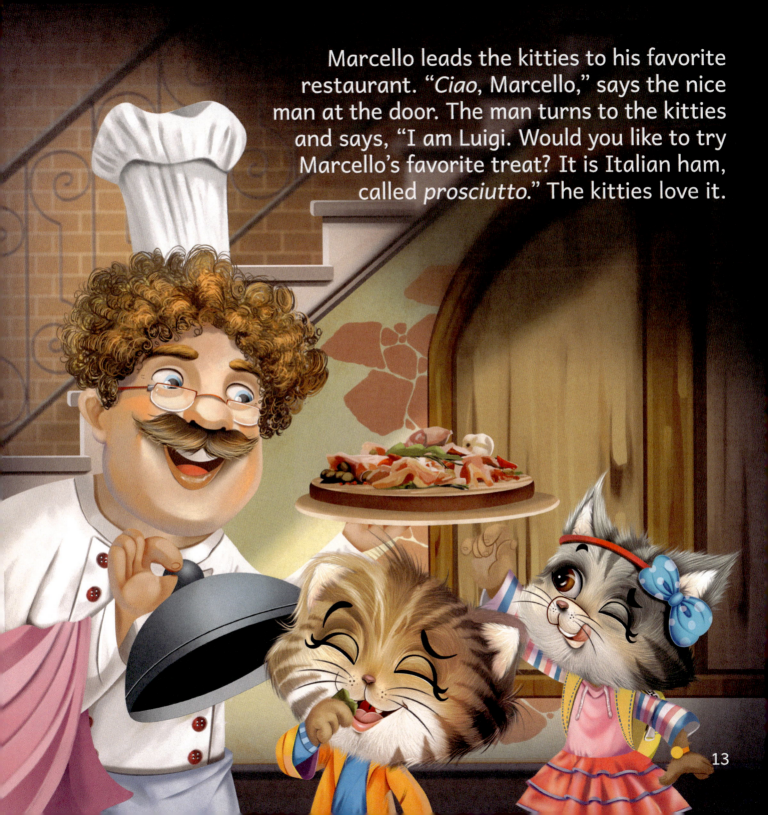

Marcello leads the kitties to his favorite restaurant. "*Ciao*, Marcello," says the nice man at the door. The man turns to the kitties and says, "I am Luigi. Would you like to try Marcello's favorite treat? It is Italian ham, called *prosciutto*." The kitties love it.

Buffy asks Luigi, "Could you teach me how to make spaghetti? I would like to be a chef someday!" Luigi answers, "I would be happy to show you how to make spaghetti. Buffy is excited as Luigi helps her put on her own apron and hat.

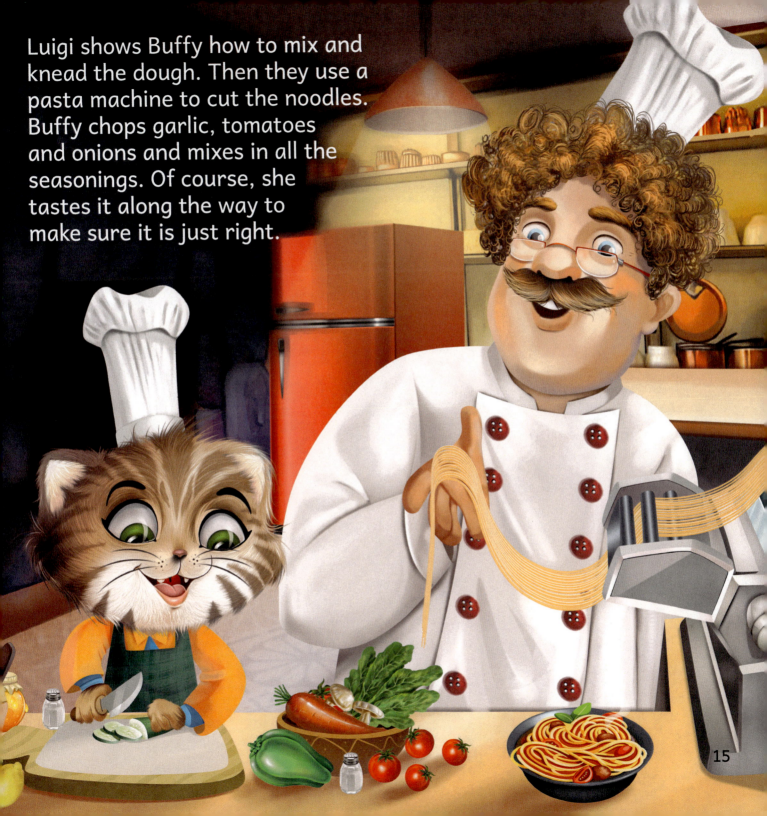

Luigi shows Buffy how to mix and knead the dough. Then they use a pasta machine to cut the noodles. Buffy chops garlic, tomatoes and onions and mixes in all the seasonings. Of course, she tastes it along the way to make sure it is just right.

"Ta-da!" says Buffy proudly! "I am a chef!" They all applaud and Sissy takes pictures of Buffy as she poses with her delicious spaghetti.

The kitties continue to explore *Florence*. They visit an old bridge called the *Ponte Vecchio*. Sissy loves looking at the sparkly jewelry in the shops.

She sees a charm with *I Love Italy* printed on it.

"I will ask Mama if I can have this as a souvenir to put on my backpack," she says.

The next day, the kitties hop on the train to visit *Rome*. "Look at that old building that is falling apart," says Sissy, pointing to the *Colosseum*.

Mama tells them that the *Colosseum* is very old. "Long, long ago, gladiators fought fierce animals —like lions and bears—right here."

Mama buys toy swords for the kitties who make believe they are real gladiators.

Buffy, Sissy, and Mama walk all over the big city. There is so much to see in *Rome*.

"It's so hot! I'm going to dip my paws in this water," says Sissy. She climbs the wall of a large fountain and makes a big loud splash as she accidentally falls into the water.

A nearby policeman scolds her and says, "No cats are allowed in the *Trevi Fountain*." Embarrassed and wet, Sissy asks Mama, "What is the *Trevi Fountain*?"
"It was built over 200 years ago and is one of the most famous fountains in the world," answers Mama. Sissy, still dripping wet, takes pictures of Mama and Buffy posing in front of the fountain.

Buffy notices a man selling what looks like ice cream. Mama tells her it is called *gelato* and asks the kittens if they would like to try it. Buffy asks for spaghetti flavor but, when the man begins to laugh, she chooses chocolate instead.

Sissy sees the words *panna cotta* on the menu. As soon as the man says it is made from sweet cream, she chooses this one. "I'm learning Italian words already," she says proudly.

Next, the kitties take the train to a town called *Pisa*.
"Sissy! Be careful!" yells Buffy. "It looks like this building is about to fall over!"
Mama tells them the building is called the *Leaning Tower of Pisa* and it has been leaning since it was built—over 700 years ago.

Sissy takes pictures of Buffy pretending to hold up the tower with her finger.

Sitting near the tower, they see a little boy. "*Ciao*, kitties!" the boy says. Buffy asks him if he knows where they can get pizza.

"Yes, my *nonna* owns a restaurant and makes the best pizza in town. I will take you there."

"What is a *nonna*?" asks Sissy.

"*Nonna* means grandmother in Italian," the boy answers.

Once they are seated in *Nonna*'s restaurant, a big round tray of steaming pizza appears on their table. Buffy dives into the pizza while Sissy laughs and takes pictures of her sister's messy face.

Soon it is time to go home. Mama surprises Buffy and Sissy by giving them each one of the special charms that Sissy saw at the jewelry store. They thank Mama and attach them to their backpacks.

On the airplane, the kitties reminisce about their Italian vacation. "We learned a lot about Italy and made some wonderful friends," says Mama. "That's what travel is all about."
"I took lots of beautiful pictures that may someday appear on a magazine cover," says Sissy.
"I learned to make spaghetti, and I loved eating yummy gelato and pizza," adds Buffy.

We can't wait for our next adventure!

Words that Buffy & Sissy learned in Italy

Ciao	~ Hello and Goodbye	
Bella	~ Beautiful	
Nonna	~ Grandmother	
Gelato	~ Italian-style ice cream	
Panna-Cotta	~ Cooked Cream	
Prosciutto	~ Italian dry-cured ham	

Other Italian words

Grazie	~ Thank You
Buon Giorno	~ Good Morning
Ti amo	~ I love you
Madre	~ Mother
Padre	~ Father

Did you know that the characters of Buffy & Sissy are based on real cats? Buffy and Sissy are tabby sisters who live in Ferndale, Washington with their human mama!

Meet Sissy

Meet Buffy

Photos by Antonio Crutchley

Please visit **www.thetravelingkittens.com** to download your free activity and coloring sheets of
Buffy and Sissy's trip to Italy!

Follow Buffy & Sissy on social media!

 thetravelingkittens2

 The Traveling Kittens

Giving back is important to Buffy & Sissy. A portion of the profits of this series will go towards charities to help animals.

Share this book with your friends!

Made in the USA
Monee, IL
18 December 2022